UNEXPECTED PEACE

Bonnie (Cooper) Startup

WestBow
PRESS
A DIVISION OF THOMAS NELSON

All Scripture taken from the New King James Version. Copywrite 1979,
1980, 1982 by Thomas Nelson, Inc. Used by permission. All rights reserved.

WestBow Press books may be ordered through booksellers or by contacting:
WestBow Press
A Division of Thomas Nelson
1663 Liberty Drive
Bloomington, IN 47403
www.westbowpress.com
1-(866) 928-1240

Because of the dynamic nature of the Internet, any web addresses or
links contained in this book may have changed since publication and
may no longer be valid. The views expressed in this work are solely those
of the author and do not necessarily reflect the views of the publisher,
and the publisher hereby disclaims any responsibility for them.

Any people depicted in stock imagery provided by Thinkstock are models,
and such images are being used for illustrative purposes only.

Certain stock imagery © Thinkstock.

ISBN: 978-1-4497-5272-9 (sc)
ISBN: 978-1-4497-5271-2 (e)
Library of Congress Control Number: 2012908917
Printed in the United States of America

WestBow Press rev. date: 06/01/2012

CONTENTS

PRELUDE

If I hadn't planted pansies last fall, I would be staring at dirt and weeds right now. Instead, the multi-colored pansies wave a cheerful hello to me as the gentle spring breeze blows across their lovely petals. How like God to create beauty in barren places, but He needs our labor; a labor of love and faith to be sure, but also patience; patience to wait for the season of reaping. Sowing and reaping always reminds me of *walking by faith not by sight (II Corinthians 5:7).*

In the cold, windy, late fall afternoon, I wondered if it would even be worth the effort. I'm here to tell you, "Yes, yes, it was worth all the time and effort spent!" Sitting at my patio table watching all the loveliness of spring being reborn, my heart overflows with love and gratitude to the God of creation.

Think of all the beauty waiting for us in that glorious city called Heaven. Nothing in this fallen world will even compare. A life spent sowing for God in the barren places of this world will someday cause us to shout, "Yes, yes, it was worth all the time and effort spent," as Jesus places the overcomers crown on our head. Being earthbound, it is hard sometimes to visualize all that God has prepared for those that love Him so we live by faith, seeing the invisible as visible and yet still not being able to comprehend it all.

Speaking a word of Christ's love to the old, frail and very wrinkled precious woman of God in the home for the aged is sowing. How she grinned a big, wide toothless smile at just the mention of His lovely name! The precious seventy-year old amputee sitting in a wheelchair scarred by life's trials and tribulations seemed to be only looking for a kind word, a touch on the shoulder, a smile, a heartfelt prayer for God to help him endure; just someone to take the time, to make the effort. That is also sowing. It might have been just what he needed to keep on keeping on that lonely winter day in the nursing home. I don't know. Only God knows but doing what He leads us to do is *always* the right thing to do. To spend our lives giving our time and talents to others brings much glory to our heavenly Father. "Give unto others as He has given to you," is our Lord's loving command. We are the beneficiaries. Joy is our reward.

I know I will see them both again. I picture one with a smooth, creamy complexion and clear, sparkling eyes again and the other running and jumping as he once did as a young boy. God will recreate them as fresh and new as the mornings dew and what a time of rejoicing we will have then. What grace God has bestowed on us to allow us the *privilege* of working in His fields.

His sun is shining down on my face as I write today and how pleasurable it is. Even more pleasurable than this is His Son, the Lord Jesus Christ, shining in my soul and illuminating my mind. What joy, what peace, what grace He gives! Walking in the Light of the world—what a wonderful way to live! How very glad and thankful I am to have waited on the Lord for this day. Truly, this is a season of reaping and renewal in my life but winter always precedes spring.

Let me share with you some of my faith walk stories beginning over thirty-five years ago.

THE BEGINNING

(of a life-long relationship)

Sitting at my little kitchen table one beautiful fall morning, my attention was captured by an old-fashioned gospel preacher by the name of Oliver B. Green. Never had I heard such down to earth, spirit-filled preaching of God's truth in all my life. I had attended church since I was a little girl as my mother had made my brother and I go, but truthfully, it did little, if anything to change my life. I'm sure it wasn't anyone's fault except my own but somehow none of it made any sense to me. Church was SO boring back then.

All my teen years were spent "looking for love in all the wrong places" and after going from one relationship to another, I thought I had finally found the one I couldn't possibly live without. A marriage transpired that was doomed to begin with. With a baby on the way and the pressures to live responsibly, my young husband decided life was much more fun being single. Girlfriends were just too much for him to give up so we were divorced at the young age of 21. Life looked pretty dismal to me now except for my precious, little baby boy. I decided I would just dedicate my life to my son and I quickly saw it would take all my effort to just shelter, feed and clothe us and I knew, surely, there must be more to life than this. I loved being a mother (and still do) but something was really missing. After a few months of being single again, I finally started to heal and realize what a mistake the whole thing had been. I didn't see any of it as "sin" yet.

After accepting my fate in life and finding through my child a reason to go on, suddenly everything came crashing down when...

The phone pierced the darkness demanding I immediately grab it off its hook. It was almost midnight and I had just fallen asleep. My heart was racing madly as I hastily said hello. My brother, Jimmy, on the line saying, "Meet me at the hospital! Dad shot himself!" He assured me the ambulance was already on the way.

Leaping out of bed, I threw some clothes on and ran barefooted next door screaming at my neighbor to please come quickly and stay with Shawn while I rush to the emergency room. My little Volkswagen bug couldn't seem to go fast enough that night! It was a miracle of God I didn't wreck or even get a ticket. I'm sure my speedometer hit at least 85 to 90 miles per hour!

Racing through the hospital emergency room door, I immediately saw my brother's ashen face and my mom's hysterical voice shouting, "Your dad killed himself, your dad killed himself!" "God," I screamed in my heart and mind, "how could you let this happen?" My dad had been an agnostic and I knew instinctively he must surely be in hell. I loved my dad even though he had hurt me deeply many times. This pain was even worse than the pain of divorce. Not knowing what to do now except try to help my mother cope, I was more perplexed than ever about life and the meaning of it all.

As the relatives gathered for the funeral, I tried to smile and make everyone feel better. Never could I let them see the horrible pain I felt would never go away. Slowly, it sank into my consciousness that I would never see my dad again and hopelessness overcame me along with a sense of the futility of life. I thought I remembered a God of love that a Sunday school teacher had tried to tell me about. Where was He now? Probably none of it was true anyway, I reasoned. Really bad things happen to people so there must not be a God who cares.

Thoughts of killing myself as my dad had done began to overtake me but knowing this would totally crush my mother, I couldn't go through with it. I did want to see her get better and be able to go on with life. I knew I had to keep on living for her sake. Neither did I want my little baby boy to grow up knowing that both his granddad and his mom had killed themselves. I decided then and there to never consider suicide again. The after effects of suicide are just too extremely devastating to everyone.

As I tried to help console my mother, I wasn't facing my own need for consolation. In retrospect, this is the story of most of my life. I was always trying to help others and never reaching out for help myself. Are you like this? Women especially seem to be. Women are always the caretakers and try to "take care" of everyone's needs while ignoring their own.

The hardest part of losing my dad was when I had to go into the funeral home and get his remains. My mom couldn't face going in so she insisted I go. When the funeral director handed me a little white box, just a little white box full of ashes, I thought this couldn't be all that's left of my dad. I couldn't deal with the fact that he had chosen to be cremated so I tried to block it out of my mind and pretend it was just a box of dirt. Surely my dad was somewhere else. No one should have to get their mom or dad or any loved one from a funeral home with their whole life seemingly reduced to a just a little box of ashes; no one.

Life took a turn for the better, at least temporally, when a few weeks after my dad's funeral, I met and later married my present husband, Richard. I didn't really want to meet or even date anyone again but there he was. I fell pretty hard one more time! He also had the most wonderful parents and grandmother in the world which didn't hurt anything and everyone, including Richard, fell in love with Shawn. I thought finally my "luck" was changing. We were married in Nashville, Tennessee on May the 3rd and he adopted Shawn as his own immediately after. My former husband was greatly relieved since he didn't want to keep paying child support. Shawn had a real dad now and life started to look pretty good.

Yes, life was looking up and I had hope again. So here I was now in my little, white frame house thoroughly enjoying being a full time homemaker and listening to this preacher call me a sinner in need of a Savior. Heh! What was this? I was a pretty good person. Hadn't I always tried to help others and keep my hurts and problems to myself? What was this fanatical preacher talking about? I did believe, at least mentally again after a season of doubt, that there must be a God who cares, and yes, I believed He was the God of the Bible, so wasn't this enough? What's this about asking God to forgive you? Anyway, I had already "raised my hand" in a Child Evangelism class my mother taught to accept Christ but I never really prayed from my heart for forgiveness. I know now I just wanted to get my mom's approval. Even though I loved the Bible stories, especially the one about Daniel in the lion's den, I still didn't know Jesus. I began to be pretty uncomfortable with the whole idea of me being a sinner; one who had, in fact, caused Jesus to die on a cross. I thought to myself, "It was all those other people who crucified Him. I had nothing to do with it. I wouldn't do something so despicable. After all, I'm too nice a person."

So why wouldn't these uncomfortable feelings go away? During the night with sleep eluding me, I tossed and turned hearing the old gospel preacher's words resounding in my mind. "Repent," he kept saying, "Repent or perish." I knew now I had a choice to make since I didn't want to die without being forgiven and spend an eternity separated from God. Repent or perish. There's no other way.

Well, God, here goes. Probably getting pregnant before being married was wrong. Probably, there's no probably to it—it was wrong! What?! There's even more? There's a WHOLE LOT MORE?! How many lies have I told? Too many to count? I don't really love people like You do? I did like most people. That's not enough? Now I could see I really didn't even like myself most of the time. But YOU LOVE ME ANYWAY? WHY?! So that's what the cross is all about. Now I was getting it! I certainly didn't understand it all but in some strange way it was starting to make sense. "Lord," I prayed, "please listen to me. I've been really, really wrong. I have left you out of my life all of my life and going to church hasn't changed me. I see now that I am a sinner, one of the worst it seems, but I heard that preacher talk about grace. Yes, Lord, grace. I really need that. Please forgive me for everything, mostly for shutting you out of my life and causing you such pain as I sinned and sinned and sinned some more. You WILL forgive me? YOU MEAN YOU ALREADY HAVE? WOW!! That's the best news I have ever heard!! I will love you forever, Lord and do **anything** You ask."

THANK YOU, JESUS!

For by grace you have been saved through faith, and that not of yourselves; it is the gift of God, not of works, lest anyone should boast.
Ephesians 2:8 & 9

THE NEIGHBOR

(missed opportunity)

What a joy was mine! God had cleaned up my life from the inside out and made all things brand new. Spring was finally springing up all over my yard and my mood matched the day.

Happily gathering my gardening tools from the beat up old garage and with a song in my heart, I plopped down at the side of my house to plant impatiens. What fun I was having listening to the birds singing (I think they knew I was saved and were sharing in my joy) and digging in the dirt has always been a great source of pleasure to me. Don't ask me why, I just know I love it. Feeling the cool dirt, still damp from the morning's dew, was just so wonderful. I thought to myself, "Life just couldn't get any better than this!"

Looking at our little gift from God playing in his playpen under the huge oak tree, I was so thankful that even before I knew the Lord, He had led me to name our precious baby boy, David Paul. After I was truly born again,

I fell in love with David in the Old Testament and Paul in the New Testament. They are still today my favorite men in the Bible. You see, when God changed my life I immediately fell in love with the Bible. I couldn't seem to get enough. I would read for hours on end sometimes getting up in the middle of the night to read some more. What a wonderful book, this Book of Life.

As David cooed in his playpen while watching the other little children laughing and playing in our back yard I remember thinking, "God, you are the greatest! I love you so much!" My life was perfect as far as I was concerned. As I began to plant the lovely flowers, the Holy Spirit started talking to my heart. I paused briefly to think about what He was trying to tell me then quickly dismissed the idea. After all, it was something I could do later in the day when all the flowers had been planted and probably a better time would be after lunch when my little children would take their nap. Yeah, that was it. "I'll go right after lunch, Lord."

You see, God wanted me to go tell my next-door neighbor about Him and how much He loved her, too. Well, I had plenty of time. Of course I would go; just later. Right after lunch, I decided, I'll ask my Christian neighbor across the street to babysit while I go share what the Lord's laid on my heart. I hope the lonely, older lady in the little duplex next door will listen. "I especially hope she won't laugh at me, Lord, or think I'm a religious fanatic." I certainly used to think that people who went around talking about Jesus were a little weird.

The flowers were so beautiful. What a great time I had planting them. My precious children were now fast asleep and as I sat around enjoying the beauty of the day suddenly

I heard a knock at my front door. "Well, who could that be?" I mused to myself. "I sure hope they don't wake up my napping children." What in the world was my neighbor, Mr. Massey, doing at my door? He looked so crestfallen and heartbroken that I found myself sputtering, "What's wrong, what's wrong, Mr. Massey?" He then told me that our neighbor, the one next door to me in the duplex, had gotten drunk during the day and had crashed her car into a giant oak tree on the side of the road going around 80 to 90 miles an hour according to witnesses. I vaguely remembered seeing her leave as I was planting my all-important flowers. He said the policeman that had knocked on his door seeking information about the widow lady told him it seemed like she was intent on killing herself. He really didn't think it was an accident since she was driving drunk so early in the day.

Another suicide! Oh, dear God! It was her last opportunity. Maybe as she sat there drinking, she really wanted someone to come give her a reason to live. I'm certain the Lord knew all about her and wanted so bad to reach her.

Now the morning was over and the opportunity was gone forever. My neighbor was out in eternity and almost surely in hell as I knew her to be a lost, confused, hurting woman. Life had dealt her some cruel blows and, I guess, she just finally gave up.

"Didn't I say something about going where You want me go, doing what You want me to do? Oh, dear, dear God, please forgive me. Please help me to forgive myself. I'll never, ever forget her. You wanted to tell her of your great love for her through someone who thought planting flowers was more important at the moment and now she's gone." Mr. Massey shared with me he had the very same strong conviction to go that very morning and share the Lord with her. How we both had failed the One who would never fail us. "Lord, please help me to never forget this very hard lesson."

Always, always, go when the Lord says go, say what the Lord would have you say, do what the Lord would you do—someone's eternal fate may depend on it.

Forgiveness finally came and peace was restored but only after a season of tears and repentance. Obey the Holy Spirit's prompting at all costs.

Be a doer of the Word and not a hearer only.
James 1:22

THE SACRIFICES

(God loves a cheerful giver)

Here I was—a young, happy homemaker on a very tight budget. There never seemed to be enough money so I babysat during the week and did all I could short of leaving my children with someone else to work outside the home. Their childhood would be over quickly enough without my missing most of it, I reasoned. How right I was! The happiest times of my life were spent watching my children laughing, running, and playing with the other neighborhood children. Sometimes, my joy would be so complete; nothing in the whole world could upset or depress me. Listening to Christian radio programs daily was such a delicious spiritual treat. Following along in the Word of God, I began to grow rapidly in the things of the Spirit. I was also falling more and more in love with the Lord each day. Seemingly small but important miracles were happening in my life and I was so grateful. Money was really scarce then so I made almost all my own clothes and the children's clothes, too. What I didn't make, I bought from garage sales or friends shared with me.

While listening to Reverend Green one day, the Lord impressed upon my heart to give $10.00 to his program so that others might hear the gospel. My first thought was, "Lord, this is all I have left from the grocery money this week and I really need a decent pair of jeans. What do you want me to do?" The Lord then spoke to my heart (overriding my mind) and said, "Give it anyway and I'll take care of your needs." I was to find out later in life that He even supplies some of our wants when we obey Him and put Him first in everything.

Trusting the Lord was starting to come easy to me, so joyfully and somewhat expectantly, I grabbed an envelope and hurriedly wrote down the address the announcer was giving. With great anticipation, I mailed the $10.00 bill. I didn't even carry a checkbook in those days and, yes, I really did mail cash (foolish, I know) but I knew the Lord would get it to the radio station and into the right hands. What a relief to have obeyed the Lord and what a sweet peace came over me!

Thanking the Lord for the opportunity to help spread the gospel through my little gift and thanking Him also for supplying all my needs, who showed up at my door the next day but a good friend from our church. Never having shared with her any need I had, I couldn't believe she was actually standing at my front door with a box of clothes she had outgrown. She was blessed with quite a bit more money than I had at the time and could easily afford to buy a whole new wardrobe. Anyway, she said the Lord had impressed upon her heart to give them to me.

As I invited her in and started looking through what she had brought, imagine my total delight when the first thing I pulled out was an almost brand new pair of jeans in my size. Wow! How does God do that? As I kept looking through the box, there was three or four more pair of jeans with quite a few tops and sweaters that just fit. I realized with a start I had received 100 fold more than I had given. Instead of being able to buy one pair of jeans with my $10.00, I now had clothes that would have cost well over $100.00, for free! I could never have bought anywhere near that much. What abundance God poured out on my little faith! A little is truly a lot when God is in it. "Thank you, Jesus!" God is truly our Jehovah Jireh, (God our provider).

Then there was the day a neighbor's dog dragged off one of my little boy's brand new pair of tennis shoes after I had just the day before given all the rest of our limited income to my church. "God," I said, "You know I can't buy him another pair of shoes right now and he's outgrown every pair of shoes he has. Please find the shoe for me and I will give you all the glory for it."

The next morning, with a somewhat heavy heart, I looked again and again for the shoe. I scoured the house, the yard, and even my neighbor's yard, but it was nowhere to be found. "God," I said again, "You know where the lost shoe is. Please help me find it."

Forgetting about it for the rest of the morning, around lunchtime I heard someone knocking at my back door. This was kind of unusual in the house we lived in at the time as I remember thinking, "Now who could that be?" Even the neighborhood kids always knocked at my front door for some reason. There stood an older man at my back door. At first I didn't recognize him as my neighbor that lived behind my house but when I saw what he was holding in his hand, I shouted, "Glory, thank you, Jesus!" I'm sure I took him by surprise as he said, "This is bound to belong to one of your boys judging by your reaction." After much laughing and thanksgiving, I explained to Him I knew God would answer my prayer. "I like being an answer to prayer," he said. He also shared his amazement that his great, big dog that had drug the shoe home, didn't chew it to bits. I told him that God must have held his dogs mouth shut! As he was leaving, we realized we had both received a wonderful blessing that day.

While visiting a sister Baptist church in Antioch, Tennessee, the speaker for the morning sermon shared of the church's great need to feed and clothe homeless and, sometimes, abused children and teenagers at their orphanage. Knowing all too well what a difficult time it was to just feed and clothe my own two children with my husband going to college full time while working at a menial job, my heart went out to him and their great needs. The Lord spoke to my heart to give all that I had which was my weekly grocery money of $25.00. I had been unable through a series of circumstances to go to the grocery store the day before and now I realized why. Our Lord truly is sovereign in all the daily affairs of His children.

I said in my heart, "Lord, what will Richard think when I tell him there's no money for food this week. Should I really do this?" The Lord kept saying, "Trust me, trust me, and see what I will do." I had been a Christian long enough to know He was totally trustworthy and would never lay a burden on your heart and then abandon you, so I gave it all. The greatest peace and joy filled me as never before and while driving home, great songs of the faith filled my mind like *Great is Thy Faithfulness* and *It is Well With My Soul*. God was blessing my heart so much I thought it would surely burst! A person can only take so much joy! The whole experience was wonderful beyond description and to this very day, I thank God for the precious memory of it.

Needless to say, our food stretched even beyond the week with an abundance I still don't understand. It reminded me of the little boy offering Jesus his lunch of five small barley loaves and two little fishes and He miraculously turned it into more than enough to feed the hungry crowd.

Anyway, Richard never said a word, we ate well and to God be the glory!

My God shall supply all your need according to
His riches in glory by Christ Jesus.
Colossians 4:19

THE ROBBERS

(fear triumphs over faith)

Hanging clothes out to dry on a hot summer day, I remember thinking it just doesn't get any better than this. Why I loved hanging out clothes fresh from the washing machine, I don't know, I just did. Even to this day I love to see a clothesline. They're getting few and far between now with people too busy to bother with hanging out the wash. Some people even think clotheslines are unsightly! I don't understand that!

Anyway, this had to be the most beautiful, peaceful summer day in history. I didn't see how heaven could be much better than this. Life was so absolutely wonderful. I felt so much love I was sure everyone else felt it too. Surely this world is a perfect place. (Really deluded, huh? But I was enjoying my temporary delusion.) Well, WAKE UP AND SMELL THE COFFEE!

Down the street flew two cars going at least seventy miles an hour, one with a flat and the other a police car. I quickly surmised something terrible had happened! As I ran from my

17

backyard to see what the heck was going on, they all came to a screeching halt. A policeman screamed at me, "Get inside your house, lady, they have guns!" As I scrambled as fast as I could for my open back door, two men jumped out of their car and each ran off in different directions. One robber ran right past my clothesline where I was hanging clothes out just a minute or two ago! I saw him run to the neighbor's house directly behind me and I wasn't sure where he went then. A woman was sitting in the back seat of the get away car glaring at a crying child seated next to her and looking so angry I was afraid she was going to hurt the poor, innocent, little boy. She looked like one of the meanest young women I had ever seen! As I was to find out later, they had just been involved in a robbery. Imagine taking a child along with you to a robbery and risking his life for a few bucks!! What a sorry sight that was! These three young criminals had just robbed the jewelry store the next street over and used our side road to try to escape the police.

When the policemen couldn't find one of the robbers after searching the neighborhood most of the afternoon, I sat frozen with fear in my little, white frame house that before this incidence held so much peace. Satan came in like a tornado and ripped my peace to shreds.

Not long after, I summoned up the courage to call my neighbor and asked if my children and I could stay with her until Richard came home from work. She said, "Certainly! Come quickly 'cause I'm scared too and don't want to be here alone!" Slamming the door behind me and bolting for her house, I know my children and I must have broken any previous records for the short distance run that day! I just knew the thief was hiding behind my garage or least somewhere very close by and I didn't want to be alone with my little children if he tried to break into my house. I had decided I definitely didn't want us being his hostages or even worse, killing us! I totally forgot the verse that says, *Fear not him who is able to kill the body but fear (reverence) Him who is able to kill the soul.* I even forgot to offer up at least a quick word of prayer for safety! Being paralyzed with fear is not a good thing! My brain was just frozen mush, it seemed!

My neighbor and I trembled together with much fear and apprehension that long afternoon while we waited for the policemen to let us know he'd been caught.

Finally, after forever it seemed, Richard did come home and let us know we could come back. The robber had been found hiding in a garage at a neighbor's house behind us and was on his way to jail.

With a start, I remembered my Lord. Imagine my surprise when I realized I had been too upset to even pray. To have forgotten the Lord that quickly and all His faithfulness in the past was truly upsetting to me. I realized He was there all the time and I had no reason to be afraid. Even if the robber had entered my house, Jesus was there and He would only allow His will which is perfect. Not to say sometimes things do happen that aren't what we would choose, just that He has promised to work all things out for our good and for His glory.

Peace was finally restored to my home and my mind. I could see how quickly I could go from perfect peace and joy to total fear and turmoil. My "perfect" world had collapsed and I realized this was a wake up call. God seemed to be telling me, "Child, you're not home yet."

Our peace is not to be dependent on circumstances—beautiful weather, birds singing, etc.—but on the goodness and faithfulness of God. He is our source of peace in the ups and downs of life, our **only** true source of peace. He is our comforter, our advisor, and our friend that sticks closer than a brother.

> *These things I have spoken to you, that in Me you may have peace. In the world you will have tribulation; but be of good cheer, I have overcome the world.*
> *John 16:33*

THE DISAPPEARANCE
(son out of control)

Many more events have come and gone but now I want to skip ahead at least ten years or more to tell you about the night my oldest son, Shawn, gave me one of the biggest scares of my life. Shawn was now 17 years old and walking on the wild side of life. He came home drunk and probably drugged that awful Saturday night around 8:30 p.m. I wouldn't have believed then he would do anything other than abuse alcohol (which is bad enough) but now I know better. This was really early for him to come home. Usually on the weekend he never found his way home until well after midnight.

Anyway, I heard a lot of commotion coming from his downstairs bedroom and rushed to see what was going on. I was shocked to see Shawn looking at me through different eyes. I quickly surmised the situation by his bizarre look and demeanor and realized he was totally out of control. Trying to talk to him was useless. Shawn finally became very angry and slammed the bedroom door in my face, locking it behind him. Nothing I could say or do could get him to open the door.

In the meantime David came home and heard all the commotion going on in Shawn's bedroom. He tried to get Shawn to open the door but, again, to no avail. I was upstairs by this time debating with myself what to do when a very agitated David rushed to my side screaming, "Mom, mom, what in the world is wrong with Shawn? It sounded like he was trashing his room when all of a sudden it got very quiet. Shawn wouldn't even answer me and I think something terrible may have happened." Now I really panicked even more and realized I had to call for help. My first thought was "Oh, no, not another suicide." I ran to the phone to call when David heard what sounded like Shawn hitting or kicking something. After getting the police on the line and giving them the necessary information, we ran back downstairs and broke the lock to get the door to open. Shawn was nowhere to be found. Apparently, he had kicked the screen out of his bedroom window, crawled out, and ran off into the night. "David," I shouted, "we've got to go find Shawn right now!" David said, "We will but first we've got to pray and ask God to help us find Shawn. He knows where he is." I was so out of control, I couldn't even think much less pray, so David grabbed me and immediately called for Jesus to take control of this out-of-control situation. He prayed for the Lord to calm me down and cause us find Shawn before something terrible happened.

We then hurried to the car and David got behind the steering wheel knowing I was much too upset to drive. He paused briefly to pray again, then said "Mom, I think I know where he is. I'm not sure how I know but I feel like he's at Wal-Mart." "At Wal-Mart," I shouted. "Are you crazy? Shawn is probably somewhere in the middle of the street about to get run over. Why would you think he would go to Wal-Mart?" I truly thought now David's lost his mind. What would Shawn be doing at Wal-Mart in his condition and how would David really know where Shawn was anyway? I begged him not to head for the store and waste more time. To make me happy, he headed for a place called Family Billiards. (Shawn loved to hang out with friends there so I felt that's where he might be.) Unfortunately, he wasn't there so David went on to the store.

As David pulled up to the front of the store throwing the gearshift into park, he said, "Let's go find Shawn. I'll bet he's around the video games." My first thought was, "Yeah, right, we sure are wasting time here!" I couldn't wait to rush back out the door and go find Shawn.

Well, lo and behold, there he was! He was standing all alone and staring at a video game. Not playing, just staring. My heart was racing so fast I thought I might have a heart attack. Gulping for air, I tried to calm down and talk Shawn into going with us to the car. I realized by this time the police were probably already at my house and wondering why no one was home. We finally got Shawn to stumble out of Wal-Mart and as he threw himself into the back seat, it was obvious he was oblivious to everything and everyone around him. He was truly in his own little world, a scary world for me to observe. I realized then that maybe I didn't know him nearly as well as I thought I did. Little did I realize the effect this sin-sick world was having on him. I'm afraid I always thought a little too positively. I never dreamed my son would do anything like this to himself.

This was the precious and oh-so-cute little baby boy I would have given my life for. Now he was giving himself over lock, stock and barrel to Satan and all his wicked devices. What a total heartbreak this was!

On the way home, I asked myself through tears and with a broken heart, "Where are you, God? Have You forsaken me? Did all those bedtime Bible stories and heartfelt prayers with and for my children mean nothing? What about each and every Sunday going to church with them and talking about You to them just about everyday of their life? What about the verse I had memorized, you know, the one about training your child in the way he should go and when he's older he won't depart from it? Lord, he's older now. What is going on?" I could see God at work in David's life but what has happened to Shawn? Did God love Shawn any less? I already knew the answer to that. I had to admit that God allows all of us to make our own choices. The things Shawn was doing certainly weren't my choices for him or God's.

This was, at least for a while, a major roadblock in my spiritual life. I felt defeated and alone for a time, never really remembering that many moms and dads go through the same thing. In fact, I felt a terrific sense of shame that my son would be going down this path to destruction. Some of my friends understood and prayed for us. Others just shook their self-righteous head and walked away. How sad that when you need support the most, some so-called Christians judge you. Yet I can remember when my children were young and so very sweet, I had the same thoughts.

Years ago when I heard of a sixteen year old at my church getting thrown in youth detention for drunk driving, the first thing I thought was I'll bet their parents must not really be living for the Lord or their son wouldn't have gotten drunk. How naive can you get? We are living in a fallen world and our children are dealing with much, much more than we had to. The things out there are so bad now I'm surprised (and encouraged) when any teenager makes it to adulthood without at least some drinking and/or drug use.

A metro policeman was waiting for us when we pulled up in our driveway. He did his best trying to talk to Shawn but, unfortunately, it was to no avail. Shawn was too wasted. A real blessing out of all this was when the policeman started talking about the Lord and how He could help Shawn. I knew all this already but what a comfort it was to hear it again and to know God had sent a Christian policeman to our home. He strongly suggested that we get Christian counseling for him and that gave me renewed hope.

David still says God told him exactly where to find Shawn. I have to believe him because we did find him there. What a miracle this was but it took several years for me to realize the magnitude of it. God was and always is in control.

Train up a child in the way he should go, and when he is old, he will not depart from it.
Proverbs 22:6

THE TREASURE

(an earthen vessel)

Riding along the interstate with my husband, three and a half-year-old son, our six-week-old baby boy and a large dog in tow, my anxiety level was slowly starting to rise. I was on my way to a whole new life, moving from my beloved Texas to Nashville, Tennessee; a place I knew absolutely nothing about and was determined I didn't want to know anything about. With a very sad heart, I had left my mom behind who had been alone only a couple of years now. My dad's suicide still hung heavy on both our hearts and this was one of the hardest things I ever had to do. As we pulled out of her driveway, I tried to be brave and smile my most courageous smile while waving goodbye but the lump in my throat made saying anything impossible.

We drove for hours in silence it seemed and every mile took us farther and farther away. I wanted so bad to just scream, "STOP! This was all a mistake! We have to stay in San Antonio and take care of my mom," (who was more than capable of taking care of herself). I realized with our plans for Richard to get his college degree and my commitment to stay home with my little children, it would probably be a long time before we could see her again and it was just more than I could bear. I felt I had deserted her but I knew my place was beside my husband. He knew his place was in Nashville beside his son, Richie, Jr., so there was no turning back.

Even our poor dog, Suzy, wasn't enjoying this long, long ride. Every few hours we would have to pull over and let her out. When we finally did arrive in Nashville, we never could get her to happily go anywhere with us again, at least not in the car. She would even go out of her way, it seemed, to walk way around the car in the driveway of our little duplex.

We were all so relieved when the sixteen-hour trip was finally over and we had arrived at my sweet mother in laws house. I hated to admit it but I was actually glad to step foot on Nashville's soil and, along with Suzy, I never wanted to see the inside of our '66 Chevrolet again. After much excitement and fanfare, we were able to crash for the night and I never slept harder in my life. It wasn't until late the next day that the homesick feelings began to overtake me and I just knew I had to book the next flight going home. "This could never be my home," I thought to myself. My home was in Texas and somehow, someway, I was going back as soon as I could. Besides, didn't my mom need me there more than Richie, Jr. needed me here? Let me tell you how wrong I was.

Across the cozy kitchen table from me sat the cutest, blondest, 6-year-old boy I had ever seen. He looked rather curiously at me (as I did him) and then as quickly as he could make his break, he ran outside to play. Like most boys his age, he didn't hang around grown-ups too long. I can't really blame him. The conversation was somewhat stifling to even me.

As I sat there trying to figure out a way to make my break also, I was saved by the telephone ringing. Naturally, I wanted to appear polite so I quickly excused myself from the room and went outside to play with Richie, my sons, and our dog, Suzy. What great fun we all had and I really hated to see it end when we had to come in and eat dinner. I guess all good things do have to end but that day just wasn't long enough for me.

I realized with a start that I might actually enjoy this step-mom thing. We hit it off pretty quickly, especially since I was a big kid myself. I seemed to sense his need to be accepted as part of our family and realized this was harder on him than it could ever be on me. So from that moment on, for years to come, I did all I knew to do to make him feel accepted and loved. Everything wasn't always smooth sailing as anyone with a blended family will admit, but the good days far outweighed the bad. From day one, Richie found a place in my heart; a deep, deep wellspring of love that nothing could ever change.

Settling quickly into our little duplex that God had provided for us, Richie would come see us every weekend. He would run and play harder than any little boy I knew. *Boundless Energy* should have been his first and middle name. I couldn't have pictured the future that was to be his if I had tried. I wouldn't have believed it anyway and it's better that I didn't know.

The call came without warning. We didn't have a clue. Richie's mom was on the line from Vanderbilt Hospital and shouted, "Please come as quickly as possible! Richie may not have long to live." As I raced out of my friend's Bible study, I found myself just muttering, "Jesus, Jesus, Jesus"— just over and over again, "Jesus, Jesus, Jesus." Sometimes words just won't come. That's when Jesus prays for us, I'm sure.

Arriving at the hospital, the first thing I saw was my husband's stricken face. The doctor had said Richie is in a deep, diabetic coma and it doesn't look good. All of his vital signs were crashing and only a miracle could pull him out of this. With extreme gratitude, I remembered that my Bible study friends were probably praying at that very moment along with Richie's grandparents. What a comfort that was.

After several mind numbing minutes, which seemed like hours, I finally found the words to pray that I know the Holy Spirit had given me. "Please, dear God," I prayed, "let him live. He's only a little boy, today is his birthday, Lord, and he's just turned seven. He hasn't even had a chance to know you yet. Please give him and us the best birthday present ever. Heal his little body and let him live. I just can't lose him now, Lord. I love him too much to say goodbye."

The grim-looking nurse motioned for us to come behind the curtain where Richie lay motionless. We felt we were seeing him alive for the last time and yet, we just weren't ready to let him go. I knew God could do anything and certainly He could raise Richie up from his sick bed at that very moment. After yet another unspoken prayer for his healing, we released Richie to his heavenly Father knowing He never makes a mistake. His will is always perfect and He sees our beginning and our end. Only God knew when He would take Richie home.

Our heart was surely breaking. Only by the grace and mercy of God could we have made it through this terrible ordeal. To see your own loved one lying helpless on a sick bed, critically ill, is more difficult than I could have ever imagined. I don't see how anyone makes it through such hard, trying circumstances without the love of Jesus in their heart and the hope that only He can give.

As we entered the little cubicle, I was struck by the fact that everything was stark white; even Richie's face matched the sheets on the bed. Never had I seen anyone look so pale and lifeless. I thought maybe he was gone already. Glancing quickly at the heart monitor, I could see that, yes, he was still alive but barely breathing. Praise God, there was still hope! Right at that very moment, much loved Bible verses came flooding into my heart and mind – verses like, *Hope thou in the Lord,* and *The prayer of faith shall save the sick,* and many others. What a comfort they were to my heart.

As I silently prayed, suddenly I sensed the presence of an angel in the room. I can't begin to explain the overwhelming peace that flooded that little room that day. Then out of the clear blue, Jesus spoke to my heart. Immediately, I knew that Richie was going to be all right! PRAISE GOD! RICHIE WAS GOING TO BE ALL RIGHT!! HALLELUIAH!

Not too long after leaving Richie's bedside, the doctor went back in. He wasn't in there long when he came out shaking his head and looking utterly amazed. He called all of us into yet another sterile looking room and expressed his utter amazement and relief that little Richie might actually make it. It seemed he had just taken a turn for the better, his vital signs starting coming back up and he told us this was nothing short of a miracle. He left smiling and shaking his head again. It was such a tremendous joy for us, we couldn't quit smiling, shaking our head in wonder and thanking Jesus for days on end.

We do praise God for what happened that day. He did what seemed to man to be impossible but with God all things are possible.

We were to have Richie for quite a few more years after this experience and it was much better that we didn't know what the future had in store for Richie or for us. But God had a plan. His ways are not our ways and sometimes things happen that don't have such a happy ending, as we would soon find out.

Taking care of a diabetic child isn't really all that hard. It's just different. There seems to be a lot to learn at first and then, before you know it, you're fixing snacks and meals without thinking too much about it. So after a short season of stressing over what food(s) to fix on weekends, things returned to normal. Our three children and most of the neighborhood children seemed to congregate in our yard. What a joy was mine as I would watch them play from my kitchen window and thank Jesus for the fun, though fleeting, time called childhood.

Around the age of twelve, Richie started asking questions about the Bible and Jesus. Apparently, his grandmother's many Bible stories and my talking about what Jesus had done for me, were peaking his interest. One Sunday morning out of the clear blue, he said "Boo," (his pet name for me), "I think I might go down front when the preacher invites people to come and tell him I prayed last night for Jesus to come into my heart. I want to know him like you do. I sure want to go to heaven with ya'll. Do you think I should go down front today?"

Well, what a question!! The joy just bubbled up and overflowed as I said, "Sure, Richie, today would be a great day to make your decision public. This is what Jesus would want you to do and I've been praying for this almost since the day you came into my life."

After thanking Jesus and much hugging and carrying on, we were on our way to church. Before the end of the first sentence of *Just as I Am*, Richie hit the aisle followed by his younger, half-brother, Shawn. My cup surely overflowed that day!

Little did we know that before too many more years went by, Richie would need the love of Jesus more than ever. We would also need the comfort and love of Jesus more than ever to survive the hardest experience any parent can go through.

Richie grew rapidly in the Lord and loved church so much. He could hardly wait each week for Sunday to roll around when he could go to church with us. At this time, his mom and step-dad didn't attend church anywhere so he really looked forward to spending the weekends with us. He especially loved our Sunday meals together. I remember almost every Sunday right as we came in the door from church he would say, "Boo, I sure hope you make your famous fried chicken, I'm starving!" My own two boys took all our homemade meals for granted but not Richie. He was always thanking me over and over for the great food, as he would call it. When he would visit each weekend, I made sure to not only have my "famous fried chicken" but also anything else he wanted. He had me eating right out of his hand and I didn't even know it! I was really glad to be able to do this for him though. That was one of the best things about being a fulltime homemaker. I always had time for the really important things in life that children remember through adulthood. We created some wonderful memories together as he would talk, talk, talk and I would cook, cook, and cook! How I miss those days!

What a fine, young man Richie was turning out to be. Here he was already sixteen! How did he change so quickly? He did have his times of rebelliousness as most teens do, but overall, he was still the greatest! We would still talk for hours on end, much more than I ever did with my own two boys. I guess it was because we would just see each other on weekends and that seemed to make our time together more meaningful. He also loved to talk about Jesus, more than anyone I've ever known, so we had some really great conversations.

I truly thank God I had so much time to spend with him instead of pursuing a career and having too many others things to do on the weekend. My family was my career. I wouldn't have it any other way then and I still wouldn't.

The next few months Richie's energy level starting taking a nosedive and it seemed he had a continuous headache. We couldn't imagine someone so young having such bad headaches and being so tired. We knew something had to be wrong—really, *really* wrong. We just had no idea what.

After a couple of trips to the doctor's office and several examinations and tests, he was pronounced with the disease that strikes terror in everyone's heart—CANCER! Dear, dear God!

At first, of course, we just knew they must have made a mistake. Richie had almost died once and now this? This horrible disease that takes so many lives and now they're trying to tell us Richie has it? It just can't be.

Unfortunately, it was. The radiation and chemotherapy treatments were begun almost immediately. The large, malignant tumor was located near the center of the brain. They called it an inoperable tumor and assured us they were going to attack it as aggressively as they could.

Almost overnight it seemed Richie started not only losing weight but also his beautiful blond hair. He endured so much more than anyone should have to. At such a young age it seemed so unfair. Yet I never heard Richie complain or ask "Why me?" Maybe he did, I just never heard him. He just seemed to take it all in stride and kept praying for a better day.

After many treatments and several months passing, he did have real hope for a better day. The cancerous tumor was shrinking rapidly and the doctor assured us things were going really well. Better than expected, really. I knew in my heart that the Lord had more for Richie to do in this all too short business we call life.

Once again, we were thanking God and rejoicing.

The next year or so seemed to pass so quickly. Richie had overcome yet another major life-threatening disease and we were so looking forward to a long and happy future for him. Life was really great again until…

The phone rang. "Hello," I said, hoping it was my mom calling long distance. I hadn't been able to talk to her in quite a while so I just knew it must be my mom on the line.

Unfortunately, it wasn't. Richie's grandma sounded like she had been crying as she told us the bad news. "The cancer is back and has now spread down his spine." Total shock and disbelief hit like a ton of bricks! I don't remember any of the conversation after that, just a heart sinking feeling of here we go again. It was so very hard to see him suffer and I knew we were all going to have to walk by faith and not by sight, one more time.

No wonder the poor guy had been having backaches and feeling tired again. We all thought this time it must just all be in his mind. After all, the doctor had said he was cured. We never dreamed the cancer would rear its ugly head again. I mean, we had prayed and prayed, believing completely for his health and well-being. Everyone had told us God always heals, *always*. I had read the life stories of many precious saints of God down through the centuries that hadn't experienced bodily healing but, instead, had received their ultimate healing in that beautiful city called Heaven where there is no pain or sorrow so I knew in my heart, they were wrong. I could forgive them though because I knew they meant well and were trying to give us hope for yet another miraculous physical healing. I also knew my God and I knew He never, no *never*, makes a mistake. Richie's life was totally surrendered to the Lord, as was mine, so we knew that whatever the outcome, God was in control.

Truly, this life is many times a veil of tears and sorrow that we must pass through but what glory and eternal joy await us on the other side. I sure got to know my God better walking in the valley then on the mountaintop and how precious He was to me. He seemed to be always telling me, "Hang on, my child, you're not home yet" and also reminding of the precious Bible promise, "I will never leave you nor forsake you, in my Father's house are many mansions and I go to prepare to place for you that where I am you may be also." So my future and Richie's future was totally secure. Our hope was in the unchanging God who is truly the great "I Am."

Many more cancer treatments came and went with Richie growing weaker each day. This was so hard on his dad and everyone that loved Richie. I watched my husband become more and more distant with each passing day. He would sometimes just sit in our living room and stare, not really watching or hearing the loud noise of the television. His eyes always looked so sad and far away. I wanted so badly to be able to help them both but the only thing I could really do was just be there for them. I did try, with the Holy Spirit's help, to stay cheerful and be an encouragement but sometimes, in the middle of the night when no one could hear, I would just cry and cry. This really did seem to be so very unfair; especially to one so young who loved the Lord with all his heart, soul and mind. Richie usually would be the one who most encouraged *me*. He would always be ready to turn the conversation around to Jesus and wanted all his nurses and doctors to know what the Lord meant to him. He was really concerned that he might die and one of the hospital staff wouldn't have heard his testimony. He lived to tell others of the great love Jesus has for them. Never had I seen one so young love the Lord so much.

Once again, Richie was dismissed from the hospital with renewed hope to live a somewhat normal life, though with restrictions. He had had so much chemotherapy and radiation treatments that a couple of glands in his brain were totally destroyed. Plus, some of his short-term memory was wiped out so we'd have to watch him carefully to be sure he took all his prescriptions when he was supposed to and give himself his daily shot of insulin. He walked and talked now like a very frail, old man and this was just the saddest thing to me.

Visiting with us most weekends now became fairly stressful. Richard seemed to cope by hiding behind the newspaper and my other two sons would talk with him for just a little while and then make their break. It's not that they didn't care but they just didn't know what to say anymore. Since Richie couldn't drive now, sometimes we'd just get in the car and head out for nowhere in particular just for a change of scenery. Usually on the way home we'd stop at TCBY and enjoy a frozen yogurt. Richie really loved these fat free treats. And, of course, he'd talk and talk and talk. I always kidded him and said he loved to talk more than a woman, at which point he'd laugh and then talk some more. I enjoyed it though. Rich and I always had such great fellowship.

Not too long after being home again with his mom and step-dad, he went to live with his grandmother in Florida. She always took such wonderful care of him. We knew the beautiful weather and her in-ground swimming pool would be so good for him. He certainly needed some exercise but the gland that controlled his balance was partially destroyed and made him unsteady on his feet. We were thrilled that now he could swim laps around the pool and with that exercise starts feeling better. His grandmother was such a great cook, we knew he'd be getting his weight back up to normal. Everything was working out so well and we were all so very thankful. Even though we didn't get to see him nearly as much, we knew he was happy and in very good hands. So, once again, we were thanking God.

I don't know why bad news always seemed to come with the ringing of the telephone but it did for me. I "just happened" to be off work on a day I usually worked when my ironing was suddenly interrupted with that blasted ringing. (There's that sovereignty of God again). I had already talked with Richard and then my best friend, Linda, so I wondered who could be calling this time as I never liked spending lots of time on the phone and didn't make many calls.

I was surprised to hear Richard on the phone again. We had just hung up a little while ago and it wasn't at all like him to call twice in one day (I would, much to his chagrin, but not him). His voice sounded terribly strained as he told me to start packing immediately, we were going to Florida on the next flight out. Interestingly enough, I had just then finished ironing the last shirt and had everything in the house picked up. I was so thankful that I didn't have to rush home from work stressed out and grab clothes and run!

I had felt all day as if something was about to happen and the Lord impressed upon my heart to just trust Him. His peace and presence were almost overpowering and had been all day but there was still a sense of foreboding. I never dreamed though it would have anything to do with Richie. He seemed to be doing quite well lately. Actually, I thought mostly of my mom and wondered if she was all right. I had even planned on calling later that day to make sure. Even as I ironed, a great sense of loss would overtake me and tears would come to my eyes. Since I normally don't cry easily,

I couldn't understand what was going on. I would talk to the Lord about it and He would just seem to say, "I'm in control, just trust me." Richard said Richie was back in the hospital, this time in the critical care unit. All his vital signs were crashing (again!!) and the doctor didn't know if he'd live through the night.

As I turned to Jesus once more, this time thanking him that I was at home and could get ready immediately, I placed Richie at His feet. "Lord," I said, "Richie is in Your loving care and I just want Your will to be done. He has suffered so much in such a short time, I know You will heal him either in this life or the next and You certainly know what You're working out. I will trust You to do what is best knowing You love him so much You gave Your own life for him. Thank you for whatever You choose to do and I will praise You in the midst of yet another trial."

Peace, such peace as the world knows nothing about, flooded my heart and mind. Quickly, I called a travel agent to find out when the next flight out of Nashville and headed to Pensacola, Florida would be and before I could turn around, they were back on the phone with the flight schedule. With only a few minutes to pack and head for the airport, Richard rushed in the door from work. I had to pray silently that God would give him grace. He was so red-faced and distraught-looking and with his already high blood pressure, I was afraid he'd have a stroke. I pleaded with him to please slow down a moment and catch his breath but he just couldn't.

We threw the suitcases in the trunk of our car and off we went. Thank goodness, the airport was only fifteen or so minutes away. Getting on the airplane was no relief though.

By this time, we had both become pretty uptight and all I could pray was "Help, Lord, help".

Finally, after forever it seemed, we landed at the airport and immediately rushed to the hospital. The beauty of Florida with the palm trees waving in the breeze and the unbelievably warm nighttime temperature didn't mean anything at all to us. Running through the parking lot and into the hospital, we could hardly wait for the elevator to take us to see Richie. In fact, we considered running up the stairs but we were both so out of breath by this time, we didn't think we could make it to his floor.

The nurse met us outside the critical care unit and said to follow her. She wasn't supposed to let anyone in at such a late hour of the night but she felt she must. "Richie may not survive the night," she said, "but we really thought we were going to lose him several hours ago. He seemed to just suddenly turn a corner and his vital signs started improving." (This was about the time we were boarding the plane in Nashville and people were praying. No coincidence there.) The nurse gave no explanation for it, but assured us he was still very critical and didn't want to give us any false hope. I still know the good Lord wanted us to see him again in this world so I thank him for the blessing. We were so thankful also for a caring nurse at such a time as this.

As I entered his little cubicle and began to pray over him, I saw a tear roll down his cheek. It broke my heart, but at that precise moment, a beautiful verse found in Revelations 7:17 came suddenly into my mind, "…and God shall wipe away all tears from their eyes." I was reminded once again that the Lord is always in control and how comforting it was to think of our never-ending, tearless joy in heaven! He always knows just when to bring a scripture or a song to mind! How great is the Father's love for us!

Richie couldn't even open his eyes or respond to us because of all the drugs they were giving him but I knew in my spirit that he knew we were there. This was probably the hardest part for me – to see him crying and knowing there was absolutely nothing I could do to help him. As his step-mom, I had always done all I knew to do to help him in every way I could but now all I could do was just stand by his bed and pray. Thank God for prayer! What would I ever do without being able to talk to Jesus? I'm glad I'll never have to find out.

And, oh, how it pained my heart to see my poor husband looking so terribly distraught. He wanted so badly to help Richie too but there was nothing he could do. We just sat and stared; each lost in our own thoughts, each one reaching out to God in our own way.

He only lived for several more days, if you could call that living with tubes coming out of him and machines surrounding him. I wasn't there the afternoon that Richie died. Richard was alone with him when he looked up and saw the heart monitor line scroll across the screen—just one straight line then another; no bleeps, just a continuous hum. He felt his own heart would surely stop beating. "It's over," he cried, "it's over!" Oh, how it broke his heart knowing his firstborn was gone forever. It didn't do any good to remind Richard he'd see Richie again in heaven; in fact, it seemed to make his pain worse. You see, he wanted to see him again here and now, alive and well! Some healing just takes time.

This time Richie's earthly body didn't get to leave the critical care unit. That poor little body, so broken down by years of treatments, drugs, and diabetes, just gave out. One of the last things he had said to me before moving to Florida was, "Boo, if I ever have to go into the hospital again, I'm going to pray that God will just take me on home to heaven. It's going to be wonderful there and I can't wait to see Jesus. It'll be great to see Nanny, too." (This was Richard's grandmother.) "I don't ever want to see the inside of a hospital again." You see, he had been in and out of hospitals so many times we had lost count. I don't know why he had to suffer so much is this life, only the Lord knows, but thank God, we will see him again. I can hardly wait to give him a big bear hug and have him show me around my new home!

The last few years of Richie's life he would always pause at our back door before going home and say, "Boo, remember, tell someone about Jesus today – don't wait, tomorrow may be too late 'cause Jesus is coming soon and they might not be ready. Now don't forget – tell someone, ok?" Of course, I'd always say, "Sure, Richie, I'll try to tell someone." "Don't try," he'd scold, "*do it*!" He always said it with a sweet smile though. Unfortunately, I'd usually forget about my promise or feel too shy to share Christ with anyone. How sad. I'm sure even today Richie looks down from heaven and waits for me to share Jesus with someone. This was the all-consuming desire of his heart. If only every born-again believer had such a fervent love for the Savior, what a different world this might be.

What I have learned from all this? That sometimes God takes even the best of His children home – not before *they're* ready, just sometimes before *we're* ready. I suppose we're not ever really ready to let someone go. I do thank my Lord that He prepared my heart in many ways for Richie's home going but saying goodbye for the last time here on earth was the hardest thing I've ever done.

I didn't want them to put his precious body in the ground. My mind kept screaming, "No, no, he's much too young. Thirty years just isn't very long to live and I want him here with us—I don't want to wait to see him in heaven!" And yet, my heart was consoled and comforted with such a peace, it was beyond anything I could ever imagine. I knew the Lord had a plan. Even in death, He always has a plan. His ways are not our ways, but we can always trust His heart.

Richie's mom shared with me that she had come to know the Lord watching his faith. Richie had been so very burdened that his mom and step-dad become born-again Christians and sometimes he felt like it might never happen. I don't know if anything else could have brought his mom to her decision to follow the Lord. Just watching him suffer and continue to trust and praise Jesus, blew her mind. She said she became convinced that the Lord must really be real to have made such a difference in Richie's life.

Time has somewhat eased the pain but I still miss him. It's difficult for me to enjoy our Sunday dinner because it reminds me of how much he loved our Sunday meals together. I'm so glad to know we will all sit down together at the Lord's table one day soon and what a day that will be! This is what sustains me and keeps me keeping on.

Richie was always so appreciative of everything you did for him and loved everyone so much no one could ever fill the void he left behind. He was truly one of a kind—a remarkable young man with such zeal for the Lord! How blessed I am to have had the privilege of being called his step-mom or "Boo" as he loved to call me.

My all-consuming desire now is just to spend the rest of my life sharing the love of Christ with others, both in word and deed. This was the primary reason I wrote about my life experiences. I just wanted to share Christ in the best way I knew how. You see—I can still hear Richie saying, "Boo, tell someone about Jesus today."

For we have this treasure in earthen vessels,
that the excellency of the power may be of God
and not of us.
II Corinthians 4:7

THE CANOE INCIDENT

(fear strikes again!)

Sitting in the auditorium was a bore. I always hated staff meetings and this was no exception. As our fearless leader droned on, I impatiently looked at my watch and wished he would hurry up. I had too much work to do to waste so much time daydreaming!

The security guard's tap on my shoulder jerked my mind back to reality. When I turned and looked at his face, all the color drained from mine. I could clearly see his look of deep concern! As he quietly said, "Follow me," immediately I knew something terrible had happened - I just didn't know what.

As we walked to the back of the large auditorium, it seemed every eye was on me. I really didn't want to be me at that moment. "Why did he tap my shoulder? Maybe there's been some kind of mistake," I thought to myself. I had no idea what to expect, only that I didn't want to hear any bad news.

As we walked together, the kind security officer looked down at the floor and said, "You have an emergency phone call. I'll go with you to the front office." "What has happened?" I managed to blurt out. He just kept looking down as he quietly walked beside me.

My husband, Richard, was on the phone and barely able to talk. He was so distraught that at first I couldn't even understand him. Then I began to realize what he was trying to tell me. "The Civil Patrol just called and said that David has been missing for over 24 hours!" (David was our youngest son and was about 22 years old at the time.)

It was at that very moment that I remembered David and a couple of his buddies had talked about renting a canoe a couple of days ago for a 2 to 3 hour trip down the Ocoee River. With a start, I realized that they had left the day before! He had always been so good to call and let us know when he had arrived home safely after such adventures but this time he hadn't called! He had already been gone on this canoe trip well over 24 hours!

I do remember waking up in the middle of the night and feeling vaguely uneasy. It was storming outside with flashes of lightening chasing away the blackness of the night but I still didn't think of David or his canoe trip. I wish now I had taken that moment in time to breathe a word of prayer though I couldn't possibly know what or who to pray for but the Spirit knew. He could have guided me if I had let Him.

"I'll pick you up in front of the main entrance! Be standing there ready to go — we've got to get there right away!" My heart went out to my poor husband. I pleaded with him to not speed and take a moment to catch his breath, but it didn't do any good. He just hollered again, "I'm coming right now! Look for me!"

Of course, I began to panic too! It seems I forgot all about my Lord in that heart wrenching moment. My mind quickly started imagining the worst! I could just see my precious son bleeding and dying with no one to help him or, worse yet, maybe he had already died!

"Where is he, where is he," I said over and over again in my mind. My heart just seemed to sink down lower and lower as I imagined the worst and, at the same time, my anxiety level was shooting skyward!

After forever it seemed, Richard came screeching up to the curb, shouting, "Hurry, get in, get in!" I jumped in as quickly as I could and was shocked to see how distraught and panic-stricken he looked. I pleaded with him to please slow down and not take the corners so fast, but it was to no avail. I really thought we were going to wreck before we could get to the canoe rental office.

As the minutes seemed to be crawling by and with my mind going into shock mode, I knew somehow I had to get a hold of myself. One of us had to have presence of mind for whatever we were about to face. It was at that precise moment I remembered my Lord.

"Jesus, Jesus. Help us, Jesus." That's about all I can remember praying – just saying the precious name of Jesus over and over again. My mind couldn't seem to form any other words.

After what seemed like an eternity of silently repeating His name, I began to breathe a little easier -- not much, just a little bit easier. It was about then that I found the strength to pray out loud, "Jesus, You know where our David is. Find him, Lord. If he's hurting, help him. If he's in serious trouble, deliver him. Jesus, I know You love him more than we can comprehend and You can help him so, please, dear Lord, help him right now." I knew then that whether David was still alive or not, the Lord was in control.

"May your will be done," I found myself praying. I also knew that if the Lord had already taken David home, now it would be all right. No, I wouldn't like it and, yes, I knew I would miss him terribly for a long, long time to come but still, I knew it would be all right. As His incredible peace flooded my soul, I remember praying, "He's yours, Jesus. He's yours. I give him to you." What a release! To give one of my own children to my heavenly Father! I never thought I could do something like that!

My heart and mind were immediately calm and then Jesus, through the Holy Spirit, said clearly and unmistakably, "He's alright. I'm taking care of him. You will see him again." I tried to tell Richard that I knew beyond a shadow of a doubt that David's all right and we'll see him soon but he just couldn't believe me. I know that if he had turned to the Lord himself, he would have gotten the same truth.

You see, I know now that Satan himself wanted us to panic and imagine the worst. Satan is allowed to play on our mind when we're walking in fear instead of faith. It seems to be a specialty of his to try and make God's children forget the precious promises in the Word and try to figure things out for themselves. I realize now the Lord was with me (and David) all the time but I just didn't turn to Him first. How much time do we waste worrying and fretting over things when all we have to do is look to Him to provide comfort and peace to our heart? He cares so much more than we can ever know! After all, He laid down His very life for us – what more proof do we need?

After arriving at the rental office and waiting for another hour or so alone, finally one of the boy's dad came flying up, threw his car in park and leaped out wearing the biggest and most welcome smile I'd ever seen! He practically shouted, "They're exhausted and they're hungry, but they're all ok. They've got quite a story to tell you!" And they did, but, praise God, they all arrived safely back home to canoe down the rapids yet again! *Boys will be boys!!*

Be anxious for nothing, but in everything by prayer and supplication, with thanksgiving, let your requests by made known to God; and the peace of God, which surpasses all understanding, will guard your hearts and minds through Christ Jesus.
Philippians 4: 6-7

THE ANGELS WATCH CARE

(flying blocks and God's sovereignty)

Running late one morning on my way to pick up a friend on her lunch hour, I said my "good byes" and "see you laters" to my husband, Richard. Jumping in my Honda Civic, I threw it into drive and started down the driveway. Richard walked out the back door about the same time and I found myself stopping to say goodbye again – why I really didn't know but I was to find out pretty shortly.

Feeling a little silly saying goodbye again as he looked at me like I had finally lost my mind, I pressed the gas pedal down hard to be on my way. "Why in the world did I stop and waste more time when I didn't even have a minute to waste," I asked myself. Surely my friend Betty was going to be a little ticked at me. After all, we have to rush through lunch as it is and every minute counted.

Driving down the narrow two-lane road, I was enjoying the warmth of the bright sunlight on this perfect spring day and I was "singing and making melody in my heart to the Lord," as the Bible says. Suddenly, as if in a dream, I saw cement blocks flying into the air and crashing down on the pavement! The scary thing was they were headed in my direction. Immediately, I saw a side street on my right that I had never really noticed before and quickly turned in that direction to avoid one coming straight for my windshield.

As I pulled into a mini-market at the corner and away from the many cement blocks now littering the road, I realized with a start why I had stopped in my driveway. It was the Lord! He knew all along that the guy driving towards me would take the curve too fast and his open bed trailer with the loose cement blocks would come flying off! If I had been just a few seconds or so further down the road, I don't know how I would have missed hitting one or more of them and wrecking!

How like my precious Savior this was! You see, over the last few weeks I had been led to pray for driving safety each and every time I would get into my car and start the engine. I wasn't sure why but my praying would just naturally seem to go in that direction. I'm so thankful that this day was no exception! The only thing I can figure is that the Lord must not be through with me yet as He detained me just long enough to avoid a terrible wreck.

Only a week before, I had another really close call and came within a hair of hitting a young teenage boy that came flying out of a side street onto a really busy highway. Jerking my wheel sharply to avoid hitting him, I lost control of my vehicle and crossed two lanes of traffic almost ending up in a ditch on the side. Over-correcting, I immediately went flying in the opposite direction with cars coming at me from all sides. Finally, the momentary shock left me and I was given the presence of mind to shout, "Jesus, help me!" I felt a "power" surge through me, grip the wheel, straighten the car, and put me in the only open lane available.

Once again, I knew it was the Lord! To not have hit another car or even flipped my own, was truly a miracle; especially considering this was an extremely busy four lane highway with cars everywhere! I know beyond a doubt that He sat with me in the driver's seat that day and steered my car to safety.

I'm so thankful for the daily guidance of my Lord and Savior, Jesus Christ, and I never want to spend even one day without His watch care over me. There may come a time when a traffic accident does occur and, if so, I'll still trust Him. I know it would be allowed for a reason and He never makes a mistake. He has proven Himself faithful time and time again for me to ever doubt His love and mercy.

"Thank you for your watch care over me, Lord. Help me to never take it or any of your other many blessings, for granted." Amen.

For He shall give His angels charge over you, to keep you in all your ways.
Psalms 91:11

THE TWICE FOUND DOG

(God cares for animals)

Driving down the narrow two lane country highway on my way home from a joyful, yet, at times, sad day as a hospital volunteer chaplain, I couldn't imagine what had tied traffic up. Not being able to see the cute silver and white Shitzsu prancing down the middle of the road, I was getting somewhat impatient at just sitting and waiting. Both lanes were stopped far as the eye could see and I imagined a horrible wreck ahead though I never heard the usual screeching of tires or loud crashing sounds.

Finally, the traffic began to slowly move again as the precious little doggie darted out of the road and towards the middle of a well-manicured lawn. Breathing a sigh of relief that it didn't get run over, I thanked the Lord. Before I could get the quick prayer out of my mouth, the dog immediately spun around and ran right back into the middle of the road again. The car directly in front of me came to a quick stop as others behind me threw on their brakes too. Thank goodness we weren't traveling very fast yet and were able to stop just as suddenly as we had started.

Now I had a clear view of a dog that was so small, I thought perhaps it was just a puppy. Waves of compassion washed over me as I frantically looked for a driveway to quickly pull in knowing someone had to rescue him (or her) before it was too late.

Once more, the dog darted out of the road and onto the grass—(yes, God does answer prayer). Flipping my turn signal on, I whipped into the next available driveway, threw my car into park, and leaped out of my Civic. Not wanting to run up to the dog for fear of scaring him, I tried to pace myself as I caught up to him. Gently and reassuringly speaking to him, I slowly picked him and was amazed at how light he seemed. I could feel his little skeleton a little too well and not finding a collar on him, I realized he must be lost. Looking like a full-blooded Shitzsu, I knew surely someone was looking for him.

Taking him home, we were greeted by my larger, blond-bombshell of a dog we call Lacey. She wasn't extremely happy about this intruder into her space but, after a little sniffing and walking around, she decided to ignore him. In not acknowledging the new dog's existence, to her, perhaps, she didn't exist which was just as well.

It took about an hour, but finally the poor, little dog quit trembling. With one ear trimmed short (almost shaved) and one ear sporting beautiful, long, silky hair, she was a sight! Looking into her eyes, I could see the milky film of cataracts. "It looks like you're not a puppy after all," I remember saying to her. "How old are you anyway?" I asked.

I sure wish God had made dogs with the ability to talk. It would have saved me a lot of time and guesswork.

Several more hours passed until she decided maybe she would try out the tasty smelling morsels of food in Lacey's dish. I held my breath as Lacey slowly sauntered in, looked for a full minute at the "intruder", then went back to sleep in the den. Wow! Will miracles never cease? I expected at least a growl or two!

My husband came home later that evening and quickly took her under his wing. "What a great lap dog she would make," I mused to myself. "Maybe I shouldn't try very hard to find the owner." Feeling guilty for such a selfish thought, I turned to my hubby asking him what we should do now.

After "they" woke up in the morning in the same bed, I could see how quickly man and dog had bonded. (Maybe I should act a little more helpless and timid? There's a lesson here, I think!)) Richard just couldn't seem to stop petting and loving on her! I then spent my morning running to this dog groomer and that dog groomer, this vet and that vet, leaving my "Found Dog" notices everywhere I could think of. Feeling I had left no stone unturned, I headed home. I could hardly wait to get home to "my" new little friend!

We had a fairly uneventful day except one thing kept surprising me. Every time I would say my dog Lacey's name, the other dog would come to me. Otherwise, she would just ignore me as she slept the day away. I would find out why soon enough.

Richard called to say he had found a missing dog sign that he could barely read. It had been posted over five months ago but it sure did describe the little cutie except this dog looked and acted so much older than the ad stated.

Oh, well. At least it did say the dog was a Shitzsu and silver and white, at that! They just had to be owners!

Meeting the mom was unusual. At first, she wasn't quite sure this was her dog (I would think you would know your own dog!) but then, it had been quite a while and this dog had an extremely short and very recent, haircut. It did have the same markings and was even the same size, give or take a pound or two. After a few minutes holding the dog and examining every nook and cranny, she decided that maybe it was her dog after all. Noticing a little reluctance still, I assured her that if she got home and looked at pictures of her dog and they didn't exactly match, I would be glad to take the dog back.

Driving back home, I prayed that if she wasn't truly the owner, she would realize it quickly. When I didn't hear from her that evening, I assumed all was well and asked the Lord to make the dogs' adjustment back home a quick and successful one.

A couple of days later and at the end of a beautiful, sunny afternoon, suddenly I had this overwhelming desire to go to the grocery store. Since this was a Saturday and I usually do my shopping on Mondays now that I was home full time, I couldn't quite understand why I felt I must go and go now but go I did.

Leaving the store, I hadn't driven too far when a mental picture of the sweet doggie came strongly to mind. It was at the moment in time that the Holy Spirit seemed to say, "Look!" My head jerked towards the telephone pole coming up quickly at the side of the road and, of all things, there was another, larger, brand new sign that said, (you guessed it), "Lost Shitzsu. Silver and white. 15 years old. One ear is shaved. Has had surgery. Needs medical help. Answers to the name of Lacey. Reward."

Well, that explained why the dog came to me every time I said the name Lacey but what was I to do now? I knew immediately I had given the dog away to the wrong person. "But, Lord, I reasoned, she hasn't called me so how do I tell her she has the wrong dog? Help me, Lord. Please show me what to do."

Arriving home, I didn't even take time to bring the groceries in. With the real owners number in hand, I started to dial when I noticed my caller I.D. light blinking. I saw that it was Patricia's number—the lady that had the dog! My heart started racing as I quickly returned her call, praying the whole time that she had finally realized this wasn't her dog to keep. The first thing out of her mouth was, "I'm so sorry to tell you this but I took the dog to the animal clinic and they told me this was a much older dog than mine." Well, hallelujah and praise God! The Lord was working everything out. I'm so glad I obeyed that still, small voice and wasn't home when she first called. Now I could match the dog with the right owner! Meeting the rightful owners was quite an experience. I don't remember being hugged so much in quite a long time! And Patricia was so gracious in handing over Lacey, it was an extra blessing! After such a joyful reunion, and with a picture in hand of the still missing dog, I turned to go when the "daddy" of little Lacey held out of his hand for a final thank you and goodbye. Putting out my hand to grasp his, I felt a crisp, folded bill slipped into it. Assuring him I already had my reward, I tried to give it back. He immediately turned on his heel, refusing to even discuss the matter.

Driving down the same road where this little adventure began, I was silently thanking and praising the Lord for what he had just done. Reaching my home and feeling "all's well that ends well," I unfolded the bill I had stuck into my pocket. Quick tears came into my eyes as I stared at a $100.00 bill and remembered that just a few days ago, I had given that exact amount to a young person that had to have immediate financial help. I learned long ago that giving out of your own need when the Lord clearly directs you, is always the right decision and, in doing so, you will never suffer lack.

The Lord Jesus Christ loves to minister to us when we minister to others and it's such a beautiful relationship. He truly is a *friend that sticks closer than a brother* (Proverbs 18:24) and is the God who never changes; faithful even when we're not and promises *never to leave us or forsake us* (Hebrews 13:5b). What an awesome God we serve! Praise His Holy Name!

> **Beloved, let us love one another, for love is of God; and everyone who loves is born of God and knows God. I John 4:7**

It is my prayer that you have been encouraged by the faithfulness of God through these true stories written many years ago now and will trust Him with all your heart, soul and mind for He alone is truly trustworthy. He loves you SO much, dear reader! All glory, honor, and praise belong to our Lord and Savior, Jesus Christ, both now and forever.

Blessings!
Bonnie (Cooper) Startup
Mount Juliet, Tennessee

Thank you to:

My husband, Richard, who has shared life's joys and sorrow and remained faithful through it all…I will always love you.

My precious stepson, Richie, I can hardly wait to see your face again as we laugh together once more, but this time, in that forever land called heaven where they'll be no more pain or sorrow and that dreaded disease, cancer, cannot enter in.

Two sons, Shawn and David, for helping me grow wiser as you grew taller and are now fully grown men. I can't imagine how life would have been without you! I would have missed many opportunities you afforded me to experience God's wonderful peace and faithfulness. I love you both with all my heart!

My best friend and sister in Christ, Linda Miller, whose listening ear and heart have been a gift from God to me for over 25 years now. Faithful friends like you are such a blessing and I know God will reward you richly for your patience and perseverance with my type A personality.

My newest friend and sister in Christ, Vicki Isham, for going above and beyond the call of sisterhood in helping me see Christ more clearly by being so consumed with Him both in word and deed. What a joy you have become to me!

Bless you, Barbara Mann, for taking the time to read my manuscript and pronouncing it worthy of publishing. What a precious, Godly sister in Christ you are. I can easily see why God chose you to be a pastor's wife. It shows in everything you say and do!

Kathy Freshwater and the Thursday morning prayer warriors…you have all been such an awesome encouragement to me over the last two years! I thank God daily for placing you in my life!

My Lord and Savior, Jesus Christ, for His grace in saving me, keeping me, blessing me, and giving me the peace that passes all understanding. I love you most of all!

There truly is an unexpected, blessed peace that God gives when life throws you a fast, hard ball and you're not ready to catch it. The Bible speaks of the "peace that passes all understanding" and it's for real. Many Christians down through the ages experienced it and you can, too! The Word tells us in "all these things we are more than conquerors through Him (Jesus Christ) who loved us." (Romans 8:37)

This is one ordinary Christian woman's story of extraordinary events as they've unfolded over a period of about twenty five years or more of walking in sweet fellowship with the Lord and Savior of our world, Jesus Christ. I have so many precious memories of His calming peace while navigating through many rough waters of life, I just couldn't keep them all to myself.

My prayer is that you will see the faithfulness and sovereignty of God in all the events of your life, He will be glorified, and you, too, will enjoy His unexpected peace!